U0064303

時間神諭
討拍拍舒癒卡
Time Oracle : Patting-healing card

安雪尹／編著 Authored and edited by An Xueyin

黃慈／繪圖 Painted by Huang Ci

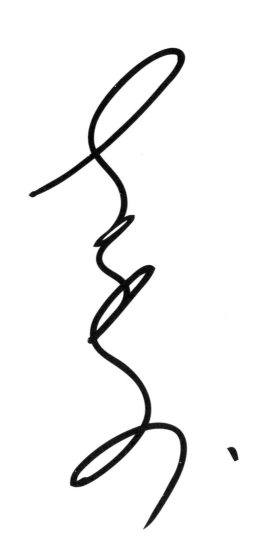

愛，令我卑微

也令我堅強

唯有相信，愛的種子才能生根發芽

——安雪尹

Love, makes me humble

It also makes me strong

Together, we believe that the seeds of love can take root.

- An Xueyin

作者序
Author's Preface

　　若患難不死，必後利他而生。

　　我與神之間的情誼，是以從事多年心理輔導、心靈輔癒、外辦在許多國家後，師父成全我在此時機藉由神之力、神的愛能助其系列套書誕生於此際，以普羅大眾較易接受的占卜方式，行解厄之實，普惠有緣之人。

　　關於「時間神諭卡」的創作之機，始於多年前自己的一個小小心願。由於現今社會充斥著無數有才或庸才的老師，藉神蹟或能言善道、包裝自己成為一代大師。其實，在我的眼中，只要不惡意騙人、害人，不行邪道、邪說，任何可以助人成長的人都是了不起的眾生貴人。

　　一年多前，我猶記得是初夏時節，連續四天，總在不經意間在望向某處時，就會看見時鐘上的數字或突來入目的數字，皆是相同的；甚至打開YouTube手機屏幕會自動跳出關於天使數字的訊息影片，不可思議的是下一秒……我這粗線條可以的榆木腦袋，竟然……傳統字眼是「被雷電擊到」的立馬抬頭看了眼時鐘，答案當然是一模模一樣樣的數字，勿庸置疑。

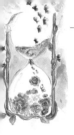

　　我還是得説，雖然和神共事這麼久，有時，這神的性子，生為人類的我，還是無敵敬佩的；為什麼呢？因為「處處有因緣，處處是生機啊！」若是你我一生，生活一成不變，那還真的沒上神師父的局呢！其實，説笑話可以，不解神的美意，可就lo了。神給了我修善自身的時間，如今，也到了該用另一種方式與更多的朋友結緣了，豈不是證了我多年前的願。於是，當下整個人突然醒轉般的彈跳起來，我不再猶豫，拿起手機撥回了台灣……。

　　結果，當然是一次比一次精彩。在製書出版的過程中，我由自己的體驗，轉向家人，再轉向朋友，一次又一次的從神諭的時間內容，得到相對事件的印證。我本具信念，對於上神師父的多方指導和呼應，除了感激、感動之外，只有更督促自己落實做好這份得之不易的神授職權工作。神授職權與我本來是位心理諮商師一點關係都沒有。心理治療是法，神授職權是能，有心境上的層第，也有經驗上的分別，兩者有互通之便，卻實質差異甚大。即便，我同上神師父出生入死（雖然，每一次出任務都是祂罩我的啦！）即便，我從小就有著與他人不同的小小能力……遇見因果，還是得自償。生命自此，雖無法盡善，但我問心無愧。

　　占卜療癒系列的神論卡，在我心目中，祂是神卡，擁有上神無遠弗屆能力的卡；祂是我在不及為眾生服務的同時，用另一型態幫助世人的卡。這樣的願力，除了神，還有誰能乘願。

　　世界上的所有力量加總，都無法除卻的，是心魔。魔生，則幻境生。或以神顏現世、或以美境迷惑人心，或以巧言魂攝思想，或以宗教迷誤本自具足。神諭卡本身非萬能，但是持有者若心正，無有恐懼，善省己身，愛人愛己，神諭卡當顯威於每一次的占卜結果。這世界上任何角落的人們，一旦展開此卡，將真心融於此神諭卡間，天道自會轉動，因果即現眼前，為您以此卡療癒方式開啟智慧，為您排憂解難。只要您相信，奇蹟便會不斷發生。

祝福擁有此套神諭卡的朋友們，因為你們真的很幸福！

記住啊！善念，不只給走在明路上的人們才能擁有。在黑暗之境的人們，只要當下立轉，「善念現，地獄即變天堂。」。

現在，容我小小說明一下，如何有效使用神諭卡。專注一念，能集萬千宇宙之力量；念中有愛，能化千萬阻擋之惡。雖人事無法改變輪迴之數，但至誠可扭轉天地之運。愛的能量不可思議，能幫助你化解不安、懷疑的心，才能隨著心量的廣度，深入問題的核心，照映出真實的自己。

現在，你只需要放鬆，全然信任，不要懷疑，專注在你即將要做的事情上。專注你的問題，放空，只專注一念。

若此際心中的暗黑能量釋出、負面認知宣洩排出，都是正常，但要在最短的時間內，將負能量排耗乾淨，之後，才能開始專注在占卜這件事情上。

後記，人是感知覺性動物。具有極強的內化自省、自我覺察和自我嚴值的挑戰學習和評篩能力，這是每個人在精神性臨界點的自

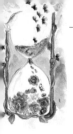

我保護與修正本能；其目的，為確保不會因為重大刺激而過度激化身體造成生理功能失衡，造成神經閥受損而導致行為失控，精神錯亂等。

　　而其中的自我嚴值，指的是「個別尊嚴的不可侵犯強度」。所以「占卜」是活的，祂會對應占卜者的各種情緒反應，直接接受到占卜者的強大念力，念力若愈真實、平穩、不帶個人偏執，則占卜結果愈精準。簡單來說，就是真誠進入問題也沒有試圖欺瞞自心，或試圖用自己的念想操縱、改變占卜結果，對於占卜的過程是正面而自然的對待。如此，占卜結果，必然有所收穫。

If one survives a serious accident, there will be a blessed life later.

The connection between me and God was established after the involvement of many years of psychological counseling, spiritual healing, and foreign affairs in many countries. Master helped me to complete this series of books through the power of God and love, using the more acceptable way to the general public - divination, to help solve problems and benefit the predestined people.

The creation of the "Time Oracle Card" began with a small wish of many years ago. The creation of the "Time Oracle Card" began with a small wish of many years ago. Because today's society is full of countless talented or mediocre teachers, they wrapped themselves into grandmasters through miracles or persuasion. In fact, in my eyes, as long as you don't maliciously deceive and harm people, and don't do evil things, any person who can help people grow up is a great benefactor.

More than a year ago, I still remember that it was in the early summer season. For four consecutive days, when I looked in somewhere inadvertently, I would see the numbers on the clock or the numbers that just came up from nowhere were all the same; even when I turned on the YouTube screen on my cellphone, a video message about the Angel Number would automatically jump out.

What was incredible was at the next second... my sturdy head with a thick line would seem to be "struck by lightning" and immediately look up at the clock with a glimpse. The answer is, of course, the same number, undoubtedly.

I still have to say that although I have been working with God for so long, sometimes, for God's temper, I am still so admired as a human being. Why? Because "there are karma and vitality everywhere!" If our life were fixed and unchangeable, there wouldn't be any chances for God Master! In fact, it is alright to make jokes, but if you don't understand God's good intentions, you can be inferior. God gave me time to accumulate good deeds for myself. Now, it is time to form good causes with more friends in another way. Is this not the wish I made many years ago? So, now my entire body instantly bounced up as if I just regain consciousness, and I no longer hesitated to pick up the phone and dialed back to Taiwan...

The result, of course, is getting more and more exciting. In the process of publishing books, I shared my own experience from the time content of the oracle to my family and then to my friends and got conformation of relative events from time to time. I have the faith that, in addition to gratitude and moving, with regards to the multi-party guidance and response of God Master, I can only urge myself to do well on this hard-earned divine duty. This divine duty has nothing to do with my original psychological counselor. Practicing psychotherapy is a method, and executing divine duty is an ability, there are different layers of mind between these two, and there are differences in experiences. The two have interoperability, but the substantial differences are large. Even though, I have gone through fire and water with God Master (the truth is that he covers me every time!). Even though I have had this special ability that is different from others since I was a child... I still have to pay for the cause and effect. Since then, life has not been perfect, but I have a clear conscience.

In my opinion, the Oracle Card of the Divination Healing Series is a mighty card, a card that has God's infinite power. It is the card that assists me to help the world with another form when I can't serve the sentient beings. Such a willingness, apart from God, who else can fulfill the wish.

It is the devil inside that cannot be defeated by the sum of all the powers in the world. The devil is born, then the illusion is born. It may appear in the face of God, it may confuse the people with the beauty of the world, it may use sweet words to control people's souls, or it may exploit religions to mislead intrinsical self-sufficiency. The Oracle Card itself is not omnipotent, but if the holder is right, there is no fear.

Introspect often, love others and love yourself, the Oracle Card will show off in every divination result. When people in any corner of the world unfold the cards and integrate their true heart into the card, the heavenly law will begin to work, and the cause and effect will be visible in front of you, and your wisdom will be opened by this card's healing method, and your problems will be solved. As long as you believe, miracles will continue to happen.

Best wishes to those who have purchased the series of cards, because you are really blessed!

Remember! Good thoughts can be enjoyed not only by people who walk on the bright path, those who are in the dark realm can also change their lives once they have good thoughts. "Good thoughts appear, the hell becomes a paradise."

Now, allow me to explain that how to use the Oracle Card effectively. Focusing on one mind can gather the power of thousands of universes, and the love inside the mind can resolve the block of thousands of evils. Although the human flesh cannot change the fate of reincarnation, sincerity can reverse the movement of the heavens and the earth. The energy of love is incredible. It can help you resolve the uneasiness and suspicion so that you can follow the breadth of your heart, penetrate the core of the problem, and reflect the true self.

Now, you just need to relax, trust, don't doubt, and focus on what you are about to do. Focus on your problems, let go, and concentrate.

The release of dark energy and the venting of negative cognitive are normal, but it is necessary to clean up the negative energy in the shortest time; then, you can begin to focus on divination.

Afterwards, human beings are perceptual animals, with the abilities of strong internalization, self-awareness, and self- strictness. This is the self-protection and correction ability of everyone at the spiritual critical point. The purpose is to ensure that the human body does not over-intensify the body due to significant irritation, causing imbalance of physiological functions, resulting in damage to the nerve valve leading to uncontrolled behavior and confusion.

The self-strictness here refers to the "inviolable intensity of individual dignity." Therefore, "divination" is alive and flexible. It will respond to the various emotional reactions of the diviner and directly accept the powerful thoughts of the diviner. The more realistic, stable, and without personal paranoia the mind is, the more accurate the divination results. To put it simply: face the question in good faith without fear of divination results; don't try to cheat, or try to change the result with your own thoughts; for the divination results, look positively. Thus, the results of divination will inevitably yield something.

目錄
Table of Contents

➊ 時間療癒系Time Healing Style

二 神奇卡解諭Explanations of the Magical Cards

目錄
Table of
Contents

來自上天的訊息
Messages from Heaven

可想過透過「數字」能與上天互通訊息嗎？

透過數字卡可清楚明白，其實「神」一直在我們每一個人的身邊默默守護和指導。當我們面對一件在當下令我們感到難以取捨，傷心難過和無法説出口的事時，你會需要用到祂。

這是一套不可多得且值得擁有具有不可思議能力的神諭卡。瞭解並妥善的運用它，可使你在任何時候都能獲得源源不絕支持你的力量、愛與守護。

Can you imagine that you can communicate with Heaven through "numbers"?

Through the digital cards, we can clearly understand that "God" has been silently guarding and guiding around us. You will need to use Him when we face something that makes us feel uncomfortable, sad, and unspeakable.

This is a rare deck of oracle cards with an incredible source of energy. Try to understand and use it properly, and you will get the endless power, love and protection from it.

強烈訊息示現

　　當你接連數天，毫無預警的在你面前重覆出現某些數字，你可以翻閱本書（時間解諭書）找到你見到的數字並瞭解它所代表的意思，和提醒要注意的事。如：「2：22」、「222」等用時間、符號、門牌號碼等重覆出現在你面前的數字，都不要輕視，要重視它後面想要透露給你的訊息。這是來自上天的祝福！

　　當占卜者，跳出51：51這張，非典型時間卡，即表示占卜者今日不適宜占卜，或是所占卜之內容嬉鬧和沒有適合的答案，故疊洗牌卡在20次內，仍然無法跳出答案。這時，占卜者應放棄今日的占卜，不要強求並閉牌一天。

Strong message shown

If you repeatedly see certain numbers appeared in front of you without any warnings for several days in a row, you can check out the "Time Interpretation Book" to find the numbers you see to understand what they mean, and what you should pay attention to. Such as: "2:22 or 222" a time mark, symbols, house number, and etc., If they do repeatedly appear in front of you, do not ignore them. You should pay attention to the messages that these numbers want to show you. This is

a blessing from Heaven!

In the process of divination, if an atypical time card of "51:51" appears, it means that the diviner is not suitable for exercising divination today, or the content of the divination is irrelevant and there is no adequate answer. Therefore, if the cards are shuffled within 20 times, there is still no answer displayed, the diviner should stop and take a day off.

注意！

在占卜過程中，跳出「17：17」這張牌卡，除為占卜者解答題外；另一個重要的意義，是上天籍「17：17」牌卡告訴你，「七日內，勿遠行。」「三日內，不得占卜其他問題，需閉卡三日。」守正作息。重要，切記！這是來自守護之神的提醒。

Attention!

In the process of divination, if the "17:17" card appears, in addition to answering questions for the diviner; another important message from Heaven is that: "Do not travel within 7 days", and "Do not exercise any divination within 3 days." Keep up the pace. It is important, please keep in mind! It is a reminder from the guardian god.

「自生數」

意指由內在力量或守護自己的天神或守護星宿星靈的強大力量，驅離厄運遠離自己與守護心愛之人。如：討拍拍卡、踩小人卡，指的就是可以由自己內心驅動的能力。

"Autogenic numbers"

means the powerful force from the inner strength, one's patron or the guardian of the constellations and astral spirits, to drive away the doom and protect the beloved, such as the Pity-seeking card and the Step-on-the-villain card, refers to the ability to be driven by their own heart.

「橫生數」

是由占卜者個人積累的福分，藉由「貴緣」、「貴人」等外在能量，為自己生成轉危為安的好運數。如：幸運卡、中貴人卡。

"Appear in the sky"

refers to the fortune accumulated for the diviner through external energy like "good karma" or "benefactor", creating a good destiny for oneself, such as the Luck card and the Noble and superior card.

「元始卡」

占卜者，若翻得此卡，若在占卜當下並無所求內容，僅憑天意擇卡之。則表示翻到此卡者，具有神緣，並希望能更精進修養自我，提升心靈層次。賦予意義：即擁有上天的祝福。

"Pre-cosmicstate card"

If the diviner does not know what to ask during the divination and gets this card only by the will of Heaven, which means that the person whoever draws out this card has a good relationship with God, and wants to be more refined and self-improving. The meaning: you have been blessed by the Heaven.

「桃花數」單卡

為此預言卡最為動人的一篇。獲此卡，不但立即為自己招來好運，還能有結桃花姻緣之佳運數。且占卜者心念愈強，能量愈盛。占卜者占卜求姻緣得桃花數卡，表示有緣之人就在不遠的地方。

"Love-attraction (Peach blossom) number" single card

This is the most appealing one of the prophecy cards. Whoever gets this card, he or she will not only bring good luck to oneself, but also has a good marriage. And the stronger the diviner's mind is, the more energetic it is.

占卜完畢後可將先前跳出的桃花數卡抽出，放在臥室床頭上或家中較高乾淨位置。若是問人際關係而得到此卡，則可在公司內自己的辦公桌上選一個自己覺得適合的位置放置連續七天，自可生「桃花運量」，非常奇妙，效果殊勝。

After the divination is completed, you can place the card on the head of a bed, or on a clean spot at a higher position in the house. If you get this card by asking for interpersonal relationships, place the

card at a location on your office desk where you feel is appropriate for seven consecutive days. It will create "love-attraction energy", and the effect is excellent.

1. 選好位置，就不可任意移動。

2. 擺放此卡時，請同時冥想溫柔的粉紅色光芒或是白色純潔的光芒圍繞此卡，直到冥想結束，能量已成。

3. 好念至，則運量生，但只有七日，不可多求。七日之後，此卡則自動恢復原本的占卜能量，並將它重新放入牌卡中疊洗。

1. Once you have chosen a location, do not move it.

2. When placing the card, please imagine that there is a pink light surrounding the card until the placement is completed.

3. When good thought comes and the love-attraction energy will be created; however, it will only last for seven days. After seven days, the card will automatically resume its original divination energy, and you should put it back to the deck of cards and shuffle.

時間療癒系
Time Healing Style

0：00

冷靜，是此刻你最需要的。明白衝動的後果，不是兩敗傷而已。而會是不可彌補的遺憾。

這是「初始之數」，也是「重新開始」之意，現在的你，要慎重審視自己的內心，不要衝動。驕傲與自尊，不要在這時候被放大了。相反的，放鬆情緒，你會發現事情其實並沒有你想像的嚴重。你只需要靜靜的覺察自己的心，耐心等待。你會發現這是值得的。

‧不要衝動，保持冷靜

Calmness is what you need most at the moment. You have to understand the consequences of impulsiveness; it's not just internecine, it will become an irreparable regret.

This is the "initial number" and also the meaning of "restarting". Now, you must carefully examine your inner heart and not be impulsive. Your pride and ego shouldn't be magnified at this time. Conversely, relax your emotions and you will find that things are not as serious as you think. You just need to quietly perceive your heart and wait patiently. You will find it worthwhile.

· Don't be impulsive, keep calm!

時間療癒系

1：11

　　要知道自己一直受著上天的眷愛與守護，順心而行，不要受人影響，未來一定夢想成真。

・上天守護之數

・耐心等待，幸福即將發生

You must know that you have been cared for by God. You should do things with your heart, and do not be affected by other people. In the future, your dreams will come true.

・**The number of heavenly guardians**

・**Wait patiently, happiness is about to happen**

2：22

· 我就在你身邊

　　我一直在你身邊，握著你伸援的手，小心呵護著。相信我，此事很快就能獲得妥善解決。聆聽自己心上的聲音，我會帶你走出眼下境地，接住幸福！

· 守護之神

· I am by your side

I am always by your side, holding your hands and taking care of you. Believe me, this issue will soon be properly resolved. Listen to your own voice, I will take you out of the predicament and embrace happiness!

· The guardian god

時間療癒系

3：33

· 豐盈

· 逢凶化吉

　　你會親見神對你的愛與照顧。

· 大天使守護之數

· **Abundance**

· **Turn bad luck into good fortune**

　　You will witness God's love and care for you.

· **Archangel's guardian number**

4：44

堅守相守的心，必能突破困境，完成對彼此的守護與期待。

・**相信他，也相信自己。**

・**幸運降臨**

神一直在身邊守護你，直到你明白愛給自主的喜悅與豐足，千金難買。感恩、感受和珍惜。

・**上神關愛之數**

・**這是對你最好的考驗**

A firm and steadfast heart will surely break through the predicament and complete the protection and expectation of each other.

- **Trust each other, and believe in yourself.**
- **Luck is coming**

God has been guarding you until you understand the joy and richness of love, and it is hard to buy. Be grateful, to feel and to cherish.

- **The number of God's caring**
- **This is the best test for you.**

5：55

· 贊同

· 結果圓滿之數

· 時機來得恰到好處

　　走吧！去追求心中所想並實現它。

· 這事，已塵埃落定。不需再掛心。

· **Agree**

· **The number of a satisfactory result**

· **The timing is just right.**

Let's go! Go for what you want in your heart and realize it.

· **This matter has been settled. No need to worry about it.**

7：07

・突破困難

改變做事方式和想法，遇見阻礙就要去克服，要知道任何事情的發生都是上天的美意，持正向觀念，真心付出，終能獲得感動與支持。

・多說無益，就是這麼做吧！

・Break through the difficulty

Change the way and ideas of doing things, and overcome the obstacles when you encounter them. You must know that the occurrence of anything is the beauty of Heaven; with a positive attitude and sincere dedication, you can eventually move others and gain support.

・Actions speak louder than words, just do it!

7：17

神會為你穿透時空之門，找回
你所失去的。

・**失去的，終將找回**

God will penetrate the door of
time and space for you and find what
you have lost.

・**Lost one will eventually be
found**

時間療癒系

9：19

· 好好活著，我已為你打開希望之門

· 你的願望，我已收到

　　相信我，偉大的神必為你平反。

· 堅持住！神會在日後為你建造屬於你的城堡花園。

· **Live well, I have opened the door of hope for you.**

· **I have received your wishes**

　　Trust me, the Mighty God will help you to rehabilitate.

· **Hold onto it! God will build your castle garden for you in the future.**

10：10

不要再執拗了，感情容不得一再傷害。

· **你要的是馬上改變**

· **你擔不起等待的後果，快點行動吧！**

Don't be stubborn; people's feelings can't be hurt again and again.

· **What you need to do is to change right away**

· **You can't afford the consequences of waiting, hurry act now!**

時間療癒系

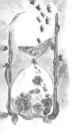
11：11

　　不要胡思亂想，幸福始終屬於你。耐心與放心，是現在的你，最大的考驗，要從「相信」的內涵裡，獲得巨大的力量，如此，你將看到遍地綻開幸福的花朵。

- 你們如此相愛，是上天注定的伴侶關係。
- 相許白頭，是一生一世，別負氣，失了原本的好姻緣。
- 擁有神祝福的你，是最幸運的人，不要做出傷害自己福分的事。
- 上天守護之數。
- 你是如此完美和幸運。

Don't think confusedly, happiness always belongs to you. Patience and reassurance are your biggest test at present. You must gain tremendous strength from the connotation of "believe". Therefore, you will see the happy flowers that bloom everywhere.

- **Your love is so destined.**
- **Growing old together is a lifetime promise, and don't lose your good marriage because of stubbornness.**
- **You are the luckiest person who has God's blessing. Don't do anything that hurts your share of happiness allotted by destiny.**
- **The number of heavenly guardians**
- **You are so perfect and lucky**

時間療癒系

11：22

不改初衷，你始終擁有神的祝福。

・決心不移

If you don't change your mind, you will be always blessed by God.

・Determination

11：33

· 搞定

· **這是最好的結果**

　　你已過了眼前這一關，幫助你的，其實是你自己。

　　聆聽自己心中的聲音，守護好你本來就具有的美善，謹守做人做事的本分，神會一直陪在你身邊指導你，並肩而行。

· **朝旭迎來好曙光，施比受更有福。**

· **Done**

· **This is the best result**

You have passed the barrier and the person who helped you is actually yourself.

Listen to your own voices, protect the beauty you have, and obey the duty of being a man. God will always be with you to guide you and walk shoulder to shoulder.

· **The rising sun brings in good signs, it's more blessed to give than to receive.**

11：44

　　現在你需要正視自己的問題，積極去完成，並督促將事情做好。

・自尊面前，真理是可以兼容並蓄的。

　　為你重視的人退一步，無傷大雅，也惟有愛與真心，可以為你獲得原諒。

Now you need to actively face your own problems and urge yourself to get things done.

・In the face of self-esteem, the truth can be inclusive.

Step back a little bit for those who value you. It is harmless and elegant, and only love and sincerity can bring forgiveness for you.

11：55

· **遇事慎重考慮，行事注意安全。**

　　這段時間，百有忌諱，需謹言慎行，勿遠遊；養精蓄銳，修善自身。

· **忌投資、合作暫緩。**

· **借出去的錢，就當做積福田了。**
　別因錢，生怨。

· **Consider carefully and pay attention to safety when dealing with things.**

During this period of time, there are many taboos, so do speak and act cautiously, and do not travel too far; conserve energy, build up strength, and accumulate good deeds for yourself.

· **Avoid investment and suspend cooperation.**

· **Treat the lent money as the accumulation of virtue. Don't be resentful because of money.**

時間療癒系

12：00

· **你需要靜心，瞭解神就在身旁**

你只要丟心上的垃圾，調整不斷和時間賽跑的自己。神正在淨化你的身體，感受來自上天的能量，這是神對你的愛。

· **很快的，解決之道，便會在你眼前發生。**

· **召喚**

你的願望，神已收到。

· **You need to be calm and understand that God is right beside you.**

You just need to throw away the rubbish in your heart and adjust yourself to keep racing with time. God is purifying your body, and you have to feel the energy from Heaven, it is God's love for you.

· **Soon, the solution will happen before your eyes.**

· **Summon**

God has received your wishes.

12：12

· **去做吧！這是值得的事。**

· **做下改變自己決定的計畫。**

　　不要猶豫，想，就去實踐。只要那樣做不會破壞彼此間的信任與重要關係。

· **平安抵達。**

· **天之美意顯現在自心的光潔程度。**

· **Go for it! This is worth it.**

· **Do not change the plan that you have decided.**

　　Don't hesitate, just do it as long as it will not damage the trust and important relationship between each other.

· **Arrived safely.**

· **The beauty of the sky appears in the light of the heart.**

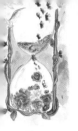

13：13

- 現在，改變計畫還來得及。
- 困守自己的，不是眼前的困境；而是束手無策。
- 讓自己一再進步的，正是這一連串的打擊。

　　去克服它吧！大雨過後，必見藍天。

- 神，一直在你身邊，別害怕！

　　神會幫助你，並陪伴你做得更好。

- **Now, it's time to change the plan.**
- **It's not the predicament in front of you that is trapping yourself; it's the helpless feeling.**
- **It is this series of blows that have made you progress again and again.**

　　Conquer it! After the heavy rain, you must see the blue sky.

- **God is always by your side, don't be afraid!**

　　God will help you and accompany you to do better.

14：14

- 我會派人將你帶出泥沼
- 打敗它！那卑鄙的傢伙，深呼吸！用力將惡氣全數吐出。
- 不要因為他人的言行，而折辱自己。

　　憂傷與低潮，都不適合你。這種折損自己，讓他人暗爽的事，千萬不要做。

- **我是偉大的神，洞悉一切不公不義之事。**

　　世事之發生皆有因果，討回公道歸因返果。你不需為此懊惱，靜待即可。

時間療癒系

· **I will send someone to take you out of the mud**

· **Defeat it! That despicable person! Take a deep breath! Force all the bad breath out.**

· **Don't humiliate yourself because of the words and deeds of others.**

Sadness and low tide are not for you. Don't do this kind of thing that hurts yourself and makes others wallow in secret pleasure.

· **I am the mighty god, and I know all the things of injustice and injustice.**

The occurrence of the world has its cause and effect, and it is a matter of fairness. You don't have to worry about it, just wait and see.

15：15

· **專注在優先順序上**

　　你需要做好，做對事情，就必須在諸多的事務中，優先選擇處理在你心目中的重要順序。

· **暗潮洶湧，謹慎處理，妥善照顧。**

· **現在改變，還來得及。**

　　別以為可以隻手遮天，神知道你一直在做的事，快改變！現在改變，神對你的愛和照顧，才能真正被你接受到。

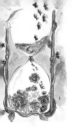

· Focus on your priority

You need to do things right, and do the right things. You must prioritize the important order in your mind.

· The undercurrent is turbulent, handle with care and properly take care of it.

· It's still time to make a change now.

Don't think that you can cover the sky with one hand, God knows what you have been doing, hurry and change! Change now, and you can truly receive the love and care from God.

15：55

· 你的願望，神已收到。

· 你做得很好，神也以你為榮。

  呵護好心中不滅的陽光，努力，必見結果。

· 好運源源不絕而來，謹守原則，富貴一生。

· **God has received your wishes.**

· **You are doing so well, and God is proud of you.**

  Take care of the sunshine in your heart, work hard, and you will see the result.

· **The source of good luck is endless, keep the principle and live a prosperous life.**

時間療癒系

16：16

· 不要輕視自己，你本來就是有能
  力的人。
· 別拖延，趕緊完成眼前的事。

· **Don't underestimate yourself,
  you are a capable person.**
· **Don't delay, and quickly
  complete the matter.**

17：17

- 回家吧！
- 相信自己，你只需要更加組織好自己的想法。
- 這是黑夜將逝，白日絢彩之數。

　　交會於白日與星夜的光子，正慢慢聚集能量守護著心力交瘁的你。放心！黑暗的風暴即將過去，你一直等待的光明即刻到來。

- 現在的你，宜善養自身，養精蓄銳。
- 閒事，莫參與；平安，一生相隨。

　　你要強大的力量，來支持自己，完成心中的目標。現在，神正在聆聽你！用真心和行動讓神來幫助你。

- 祈禱！

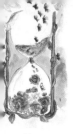

- **Go home!**
- **Believe in yourself, you just need to organize your ideas better.**
- **This is the number of that the night will pass and the daylight will shine.**

The photon that meets in the day and the starry night is slowly gathering energy to guard your exhausted heart and soul. Rest assured! The dark storm is about to pass, and the light you have been waiting for is coming.

- **Now you should conserve energy, build up strength, and accumulate good deeds for yourself.**
- **Don't mind other people's business, and peace will stay forever.**

You need a powerful force to support yourself and accomplish your goals. God is listening to you right now! Let them help you with your heart and your actions.

- **Say your prayers!**

18：18

- 要知道有人正在等著你，將心放下，就能看見。
- 堅持，必帶來甜美的收獲。

- You should know that someone is waiting for you, let your guard down and you will see.
- Perseverance will bring sweet harvest

19：19

· 你需要在濁塵中，保持清明。

　圍繞在你身邊的聲音，真真假假，敞開心靈，放下利慾；神會幫助你找到正確的方法，去完成你心中所想。

· **用愛去包容，去理解，去體現，你會發現，操再多的心，遠不如你一句真心體己的話，一個溫柔的擁抱。**

· **用人之道如用兵。**

　團結是持續推進的力量，誠信、體恤和魄力，則是驅動馬鞭的魂。

· **You need to keep yourself unspotted from the world.**

There are real and false voices around you, open your mind and let go of your desires; God will help you find the right way to accomplish what you wish for.

· **Use your love to tolerate, to understand and to reflect, you will find that no matter how much you care, it is not as useful as thoughtful words, or a gentle hug.**

· **Treat all people as in the military.**

Unity is the power of continuous advancement. Integrity, compassion and courage are the souls that drive the whip.

時間療癒系

19：49

· **不可避免做出選擇**

　　謹守你的心，你的良善，你的道德。檢視自己的短處，彰顯以德，你必能得到意想不到的收獲。

· **變化之數**

· **It is inevitable; you have to make a choice**

　　Keep your heart, your goodness and your morality. Examining your own shortcomings and highlighting your virtues, you will be able to get unexpected gains.

· **The number of changes**

20：20

· **停止悲傷並振作**

　　傷心並做下立即改變，逝者安息，而你的前途一片光明。珍惜眼前，握住幸福。

· **注意身體給你的訊息。**

· **Stop sorrow and cheer up**

Stop sorrow and make immediate changes, may the dead rest in peace, and your future is bright. Cherish the moment and hold onto the happiness.

· **Pay attention to the message that the body gives you.**

22：22

你做到，幸運便回來，失去的，正是不合適自己的。失去錯誤的，才能獲得更好的。

· 逆轉之數。

· 失去怎知不是獲得。

· 戒掉迷失本性的。

If you can do it, luck will come back. The one that lost is just not suitable for you; let go of the mistakes, you can then gain a better life.

· **The number of reversal**

· **A loss might be a blessing in disguise.**

· **Get rid of the lost nature**

23：23

· **命定之數**

· **終於歸來**

　　你的守護之神，愛你所愛，重你所重，好好安頓自己這顆心，你已遇見最好的。

· **你已經得到最好的。**

· **The number of destiny**

· **Finally returned**

　　Your guardian god, love the one you love, pay attention to the one you care, settle down your heart, because you have met the best one.

· **You have got the best.**

時間療癒系

51：51

本上神白日飛升，實無暇翻閱你（妳）的奏請。

既然，今日不宜占卜心事，許是好事多磨，或是你（妳）根本就不要靠本上神來幫助你（妳）解決問題。

或許是這裡，沒有你要的答案。也或許，明日再試試吧！

God is practicing moral teachings at the moment, and really have no time to read your petitions.

Since it's not a good time to practice divination today, it could be a good thing, or you don't even have to rely on God to help solve the problem.

Maybe there is no answer for you here. Or maybe you can try again tomorrow!

神奇卡解諭
Explanations of the Magical Cards

1.
穿梭卡
Shuttle card

擁有此張卡，猶如擁有了「改變現下情境」的神祕力量。

「穿梭卡」帶你穿越你心中掛記的當下與過去。

三日內，此事必得解釋，結果必定朝好的方向進行。

但推動此卡能量向前的力量，必是你已經明白是非與因果，愛與寬恕。

Having this card is like having the mysterious power of "changing the status quo".

The "shuttle card" can take you through the current and the past of your heart.

Within three days, the matter will be explained, and the result must be in a good direction.

However, to push the energy of this card forward must be that you already understand right and wrong, cause and effect and love and forgiveness.

穿梭卡 *Shuttle card*

2.
老實卡
Honest card

「呵呵」！翻到這張卡，只能説你是福星高照，眾神守護的幸運兒了。

今天，還是別出門了吧！

若現在的你人在外，占卜結束後，就馬上回家吧！

跳翻出這張牌卡的機率，只有百分之二，為此請您相信這是你的守護之神要求你如此做的。

"Ha-ha"! If you get this card, it can only say that you are a lucky star protected by God.

Don't go out today!

If you are outside now, go home immediately after the divination is done!

The odd of getting this card is only 2%. And please believe that this is what your guardian god asks you to do.

老實卡 *Honest card*

2.老實卡Honest card / 71

3.
大快人心卡
Gratifying card

「既然想，就去做吧！」

你的請求，神已瞭解。明白你是理性的人，不會去做損己害人和危害健康的事。

長久的積怨，放在心中，猶如烏雲遮蔽日月，讓原本如星辰明亮的你蒙上灰塵。神現在允許你重新出發並親手為你撢去灰塵。明日晨起，你就會明顯感受到神的愛能豐沛你的心靈。

"If you want to, just do it!"

God understood your request. They know that you are a rational person and will not do anything to harm others and health.

Long-lasting grievances are placed in the heart, like dark clouds covering the sun and the moon, letting you who are supposed to be as bright as a star, to be covered with dust. God now allow you to start over again and personally brush away the dust for you. From tomorrow morning, you will clearly feel that the god's love can enrich your heart.

大快人心卡 *Gratifying card*

3.大快人心卡Gratifying card / 73

4.
討拍拍卡
Patting card

　　將最近積聚在心中、身上、家裡、工作職場等處的穢氣，一拍即光！

　　首先，請占卜此卡者，雙手拍三下，之後由頭、肩膀、胸口、肚子、大腿、小腿等從上到下用手拍淨。此動作非常重要，這表示神將藉由你的心靈力量，藉由您的雙手拍淨穢氣、煞氣、衰氣。

　　※拍淨的過程中，務必專注，不可嬉笑，念力愈強，效力愈大，這是專注一念的能量法則。

　　※若是自覺家中有污穢之氣藏匿，占卜此卡24小時內，得持乾淨不曾使用過的毛巾，在空間的每個角落拍去、拍淨。完成後，請用鹽巴將毛巾搓洗，之後仍然可如常使用。

Let's flap away the bad luck that has recently accumulated in your heart, body, home, workplace, etc.!

First of all, if you get this card, please clap your hands three times, and then pat your head, shoulders, chest, stomach, thighs, calves, etc., from top to bottom. This action is very important, which means that God will drive away bad luck through your spiritual strength and your hands.

※ In the process of purification, be sure to concentrate, not to smile and grimace. The stronger the mind, the greater the effectiveness, this is the energy law of focusing on one thought.

※ If you notice that there is filthy air in your home, you can wipe every corner of the house with a clean and unused towel within 24 hours of getting the card. When finished, please wash the towel with salt and then use it as usual.

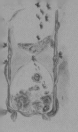

討拍拍卡 *Patting card*

5.
踩小人卡
Step-on-the-villain card

「踩吧！」用力踩！（踩小人出氣卡）

你受氣了吧？盡情宣洩不愉快的情緒，把氣踩順了，禍患便也遠離了。

神意美妙，但占卜者意念不得傷人，否則，力量會反噬自己，禍不單行。例如：占卜者可以說：「XXX，滾離我。」但不能說：「XXX，去死吧！」在這裡，這是去除霉運、衰氣大忌，一定切記！

※若占卜者心中占卜時是為他人所求，獲得此卡，便是望你能助對方一臂之力，為他驅趕小人。例如：占卜者可先將此出氣卡丟擲在地上。「衰氣快走，快遠離XXX，現在，馬上。」之類的口令，再用腳狠踩出氣卡數下（亦可邊踩邊下口令）「衰氣走，不要再跟隨我。」

※最後，收卡時，請先在出氣卡上拍七下，去除記憶，再重新放入牌卡內。（重要！）

神奇卡解諭

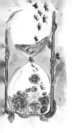

"Step on it! Harder! (Like hitting on a punching bag)

You are so angry! Let's vent your unpleasant emotions out; once your breath is smooth, your troubles will be far away.

God's intention is good; therefore, the diviner's thought cannot hurt people. Otherwise, the power will counterattack you, and the disaster will follow. For example, the diviner can say: "xxx, stay away from me." But you cannot say: "xxx, go to hell." In here, it is to remove the bad luck, not to curse others! You must remember that!

※ If the diviner is practicing the divination for the sake of another person, once the diviner obtains this card, it is hoped that you, the diviner, can help the other get away from the villain.

For example, a diviner can throw this card to the ground, and say something like: "Bad luck, go away from xxx, now, right now.", then step hard on the card with your foot for several times (you can also step on the card and say the command at the same time): "Bad luck go away, don't follow me."

※ Finally, when collecting the card, please pat the card seven times to erase the memory, and then put it back into the box. (Important!)

踩小人卡 *Step-on-the-villain card*

5.踩小人卡Step-on-the-villain card / 79

6.
桃花數
Love-attraction (Peach blossom) number

這是全套牌卡中，唯一不屬於人間的數字卡。

「桃花數」卡，具有不可思議的能量。是上天給人們的祝福，也是禮物。

占卜姻緣者，自然合泰，神仙眷侶事能和合。

占卜人際關係者，此卡諭為貴人在旁必得相助。

占卜其它者，獲此卡，如獲上天恩賜的福氣，幫助您逢凶化吉，心想事成，財源定進。

This is the only card in the whole set that does not belong to human society.

The " Love-attraction (Peach blossom) number " card has incredible energy.

This card means that it is a blessing from God and it is a gift, too.

The diviner who is seeking for a good marriage will eventually get one as a golden couple does.

The diviner who is seeking for good relationships will be assisted by benefactors. The diviner who is seeking other answers will get the blessing from Heaven, turn bad luck into good fortune, have your wishes come true, and have steady financial resources.

桃花數
Love-attraction (Peach blossom) number

6.桃花數Love-attraction (Peach blossom) number

7.
宣洩卡
Unbosoming card

「說對了吧！」此時的你，確實要好好抒發心裡的委屈了。

神知道你心中的苦，但是要如何告訴你，在不久的將來，你會因為歷此磨難而終將獲得幸福！

神知道你聽不見祂的聲音，因此以此牌卡告訴你，不要難過，不要衝動，勿因一時氣憤盲目做下決定。遵從神的指引，冷靜。

現在的你，不是孤獨的，慈愛的神正在你身邊陪伴著你。

你可以小小任性，但一定要珍惜自己，因為神如此看重你。

堅持信念，走正確的道路，禍已遠離，愛必呵護著你。

"I'm right, am I not?" At this point, you really need to express your grievances!

God knows the bitterness in your heart, but how to tell you that in the near future, you will eventually gain the happiness because of this hardship!

God knows that you can't hear his voice, so he uses this card to tell you not to be upset, the momentary anger will always pass; follow your own heart, do not impulsively make decisions.

You are not alone now, and the loving God is with you by your side.

You can be willful, but you must cherish yourself, because God values you so much.

Adhere to the belief, take the right path, the disaster is far away, and love will protect you.

宣洩卡 *Unbosoming card*

7.宣洩卡Unbosoming card / 85

8.
魔鏡卡
Magical mirror card

「美醜不在華美衣飾，而在心靈。」（魔鏡卡諭）

魔由境地生，每日照鏡而不自知。現在的你，對擇選掙扎。神之意，「一切萬物，皆是表相，唯賢德與真心難尋。」鏡中照見人的胖瘦，卻不能照映出貪婪與美好。

※你是自信的，因為這份自信為你帶來不同能量。要謹守自心安定，才能避開禍事，讓好的緣分進入生活中。

"Beauty or ugliness is not about having gorgeous clothes, it is about having the purest heart." (Metaphor of magical mirror)

The devil is born by the realm, and you look at the mirror every day without knowing it. Now you are struggling with choices. The meaning from God, "All things are appearances, and virtues and truths are hard to find." A mirror can reflect whether a person is fat or thin, but it cannot reflect greed and beauty.

※ You are confident, and this confidence can bring you different energy. To be self-satisfied, you can avoid the disaster and let the good fate enter your life.

魔鏡卡 *Magical mirror card*

8.魔鏡卡Magical mirror card / 87

9.
風暴卡
Storm card

丟掉負面的想法，拒絕紛亂的訊息。現在的你，要「冷靜」。

你擁有其他人所沒有的感知力，只要你願意，靜心重拾能力，你就能夠得到你想要的。

※風暴卡，有「機會來臨」之意，風暴至，考驗至，卻是為您鋪設更好的不久將來。

「勇敢接受挑戰，沉著應付，風暴之後，必見晴空萬里。」

Lose negative thoughts and reject chaotic messages. Now you have to be "cool".

You have the power of perception that no one else has, and you can get what you want, as long as you are concentrated and willing to regain the power.

※ The storm card has the meaning of "opportunity is coming"; the storm is coming, the test is up, but it is building a better future for you.

"Bravely accept the challenge, face it calmly, and after the storm, you will see the clear sky."

風暴卡 *Storm card*

10.
災星卡
Disaster card

「災星至，路上行人趨避之。」

當你拿到這張牌卡時，說明災禍已近臨身邊。您的守護神正安排有緣之人，為你避禍。

這一段時間（約莫14天）應避免前往高山水澤處、山丘或海邊。切記！

於此期間，在外盡量於晚上九點前回到家中，靜待這一段時間過去。

※另者，卡諭另意為：謹言慎行，亦有「財損」之虞。所以須「慎防小人」，也需謹慎評估與人投資合作相關事宜，占卜者若關於「投資」、「合作」問題，此牌卡解諭：不宜，或少量投資以趨避風險、降低財損機會。

"The disaster is coming, and the pedestrians are avoiding it."

When you get this card, it means that the disaster is near. Your guardian god is arranging a fated person for you to help you avoid trouble.

During this period of time (about 14 days), you should avoid going to the mountains, the hills or the sea. You must remember!

During this period of 14 days, try to return home before 9:00 pm.

※ In addition, the card also implies: be cautious, there are also concerns about " financial loss". Therefore, it is necessary to take "precaution against villains" and to carefully evaluate matters related to cooperate with others in investment. If the diviner asks about "investment" or "cooperation", this card will be interpreted as "not appropriate". Or you can conduct a small amount of investment to avoid risks and reduce financial losses.

神奇卡解諭

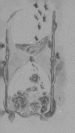

災星卡 *Disaster-card*

11.
逆轉卡
Reverse card

「自生數」、「橫生數」等牌卡能量，都不如「逆轉卡」來得強大，因為這是神賦能量。

拿到此牌卡，無論你是否有感知或同意否，占卜到此卡的同時，命運之神已自動將您的「厄」調轉為「安」，此機制已經轉動。這是因為你天性中的善良受到眾神的呵護。

故，釋放「改變」厄運的能量。恭喜你！也祝福你順遂、平安。

The energy of the card of "Autogenic numbers", or "Accumulative numbers" is not as powerful as the Reverse card, because its energy is given by God.

At the same time as you get this card, whether you have any perception or consent, the god of fate has automatically transferred your "bad luck" to "safe". This mechanism has already activated. It is because the goodness of your nature is received by the gods.

Therefore, the energy of "changing" bad luck is released. Congratulations! Also wish you a smooth and peaceful life.

逆轉卡 *Reverse card*

12.
中貴人卡
Noble and superior card

「中貴人」，權勢特別大的顯貴之人，通常指達官顯貴，身奉官祿的人。

跳出此卡，代表您將有「升官」之跡象或是近日有「財帛」至，是雙喜臨門之運勢。

※若占卜者剛剛產子，那麼恭喜您，您所誕之子，乃為貴子，
　當用心栽培，細心教養，未來前途不可限量。

"Noble and superior" means a noble person who is particularly powerful.

Usually refers to the person who is up to the official and is a member of the government officials.

If you get this card, you will have the sign of "get promoted" or be "wealthy" in the near future, which is the fortune of double blessing.

※ If the diviner is just giving birth, congratulations, the child you
　just have is a noble one. You should cultivate and educate the
　child with care, and the future of the child cannot be limited.

中貴人卡 *Noble and superior card*

13.
元始卡
Pre-cosmicstate card

　　由「黑」與「白」共同建構而成的牌卡。其境,表示「無極」乃混元之數。其意,表示「生」與「滅」的交互消長,具「正陽極」和「正陰極」之道德能量。

※若是生病之人,持問獲得此卡,表示:都有可能也都沒有可能之意,需由自生力量,跳脫現狀,惟感神之美意,占卜此卡者,自然有因緣,求取改變,不能放棄。

※元始卡諭:這是來自上天的告誡,「放下現在正在或正欲做的事,那不是適合你做的事,遠離影響你正常工作、正常生活的人。你必須堅強面對挫折,體會困難,才能重生。而我,愛護你的神,始終在你身邊,曾經,你忘了我,現在以神之名,你要想起我來,並將你交給神,洗去過去一切重新開始。相信我,我會在你身邊指導你。」

It is a card constructed by "black" and "white", which means that "unlimited" is the number of mixed elements (universe) by its context; and the interaction between "life" and "extinction" has the moral energy of "positive" and "negative" by its meaning.

　　※ If the diviner is ill, and get this card, it means that everything is possible or not possible. You need to be self-motivated to escape the status quo. Only when you, the diviner, feel the beauty of God can naturally have a predestined relationship to seek for a change, and cannot give up.

　　※ Metaphor of the Primordial beginning card: This is a warning from Heaven. "Let go of what you are doing or are planning to do because it is not something that is right for you; get away from those who affect your normal work and life, face up to setbacks and experience difficulties so you can then be born again. And I, the God who loves you, is always by your side; once, you had forgotten me, now I am in the name of God, asking to think of me and give you to God, wash away all the past and restart. Believe me, I will guide you by your side."

13.元始卡Pre-cosmicstate card / 98

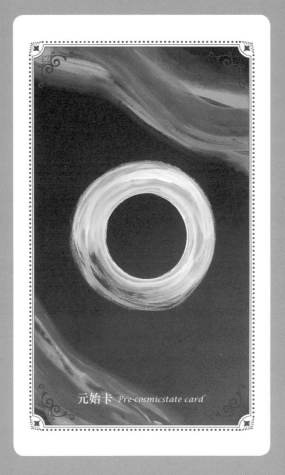

元始卡 *Pre-cosmicstate card*

13.元始卡Pre-cosmicstate card / 99

14.
幸運卡
Lucky card

「你是極其幸運之人。」

擁有此卡，即表示風雨過，春回大地果碩累累之意。

你的努力，終將獲得豐美的收獲。

※你的方向是正確的，神會支持你完成。

"You are extremely lucky"

With this card, it means that the wind and rain have passed, and the spring is back to the earth.

Your efforts will eventually yield a rich harvest.

※ Your direction is correct and God will support you to complete it.

幸運卡 *Lucky card*

神奇卡解諭

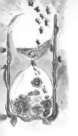

15.
異空卡
Savior card

「擁有神賦能量的你」要相信自己，始能克服所有的挑戰。

發生在你周邊的，都是考驗，你必須過關。

珍惜你守護和守護你的人，記住！偉大的神，一直陪伴在你的身邊，同你感受你所感受的一切。

※不愧心，不妄心；愛，必成就利他。相愛之人，必能相守；
　這是我們最初約定。

"You who have the power of God" must believe in yourself and overcome all challenges.

What happens around you is a test, and you have to pass.

Remember! Cherish the people you guard and guard you! The great God is always with you, and feels everything you feel.

※ Don't be ashamed and uneasy, and don't underestimate yourself. Love will achieve altruistically. Those who love each other will be able to stand together; this is our initial agreement.

異空卡 Savior card

16.
解憂卡
Solution card

你現在所擔心的事，馬上就能獲得解決。

因為你與神的連結如此密切，神愛你如子，不會丟下你，更不會捨棄你。

原諒那些傷害你的人，你的事，神已為你默默記在心中。

只等時機到來，必能因果兩散。你要相信，一切的發生，都是美意，都有其深意，讓你藉此而能躍升更寬廣的視界，使自己成為更美好的人。其目的，在於幫助你能看穿事情的本末，學習寬恕與善待，堅守住你的真心，孩子！神會一直守候在你身邊，直到你成功脫出困境，遠離心魔，享受感恩當下的幸福！即明白神會一直為你排憂解難，因為本自具足的你，如此美好。

What you are worried about right now can be solved immediately.

Because your connection with God is so close, God loves you and sees you as one of his children, he will not leave you, and he will not give up on you.

Forgive those who had hurt you, God has silently remembered all your sufferings.

Just waiting for the opportunity to come, you will be able to dissipate cause and effect. You have to believe that everything happens for a beautiful reason, and it has its deep meaning, so that you can leap into a broader vision and make yourself a better person. Its purpose is to help you see through things, and learn to forgive and be kind. Keep your true heart, my child! God will always be waiting for you until you succeed in getting out of trouble, staying away from the demons, and enjoying the happiness of gratitude! You need to understand that God will always solve problems for you because you are so good.

解憂卡 *Solution card*

時間神諭：討拍拍舒癒卡

關於時間神諭卡療癒意義
About the healing meaning
of the Time Oracle: Patting-healing card

　　每一張都是獨立而特別的，為了更能籍圖像激盪深層意像，引起人與卡諭互通能量，達到彼此感動，感受以療癒心靈，故作者與繪者在經過多次溝通與深談後，啟發心靈、覺知，創繪了獨一無二兼具諭意與療癒的時間卡。

　　Each card is independent and special. In order to better agitate deep image via pictures, inducing the energy exchange between the person and the card metaphors, and reaching each other to heal the soul, after many deep discussions which had inspired the mind and consciousness, the author and the painter created a unique set of time cards that is both moral and healing.

（一）穿梭卡

　　「你永遠不會知道，下一秒你會發生什麼？你也不會知道，明天，你會成為什麼樣的人？」

　　多重宇宙的神祕，不是僅有念力可以傳導使之變化，還有許多人類未知可以突破穿越的密碼存在。

我的夢想可以成真，你的夢想可以實現。因為願意相信，「凡事都有可能」。或許，沒有非凡的能力，來成就非凡。但是我有夢，我可以想像，我可以讓自己快樂，所以，我當然可以使自己成為想成為的人。每一天，早晨一睜開眼睛，人生就會充滿無數的可能。祝福你，祝福我們所有人。

(1) Shuttling card

You will never know what will happen to you in the next second?

You won't know what kind of person you will be tomorrow.

The mystery of the multi-universe, not only the power of thought can be transmitted to make it change, but there are still also many unknown secret codes existed that human beings can break through.

My dreams can come true, and so do yours. Because I am willing to believe that "everything is possible." Perhaps, there is no extraordinary ability to achieve extraordinariness. But I have a dream, I can imagine, I can make myself happy, so of course, I can make myself to become a person I want to be. Every morning when you open your eyes, life will be filled with countless possibilities. Bless you and bless all of us.

（二）老實卡

「你感受壓抑嗎？」尤其是現狀的現實是「你暫時無法改變，你清楚，但卻又無力改變現狀。」

其實，這僅是短暫的過程，抗拒並不能為你帶來更好的結果，為何不欣然接受這短暫的約束。環境不能改變，但是心境可以。動手做點讓自己開心的事，變化家中布置的品味，自己仍然是最有魅力的人。

(2) Honest card

Do you feel depressed? Especially when the reality of the status quo is that you can't change for the time being; you understand it clearly, but you can't change the status quo.

In fact, this is only a short-term process. Resisting does not bring you better results. Why not accept this short-term constraint. The environment cannot be changed, but the mood can be. Do something to make yourself happy, change the taste of the home decor, and let yourself still be the most attractive person.

（三）大快人心卡

「放下吧！你無法掠奪我心愛的人。」

充滿聖經寓意的故事，在融合東西文化中非關宗教領域裡的表現，是我個人所喜歡時間套卡中的圖畫之一。充滿愛與邪惡的對抗，母親純然的祈求與真誠渴望神降臨助其奪回孩子，這樣赤裸裸的心情，感動了我。誠如牌卡所論：神會消滅一切邪惡，重振正義。只要你是正確的，就義無反顧去闖吧！

(3) Gratifying card

"Give up! You won't be able to rob my beloved."

The story full of the meaning of the Bible, in the fusion of the East and West culture in the non-religious field, is one of the pictures I personally like in this set of time cards. In the confrontation between love and evil, a mother's pure praying and sincere desire for God to help her recapture the child, such a naked mood, moved me. As the card explains, God will destroy all evil and reinvigorate justice. As long as you are correct, don't hesitate to explore!

（四）討拍拍卡

漫天飛雪，枯枝影落，在一片蒼茫中，四周無人，只有落雪和呼嘯而過的風聲陪伴自己；寂靜地，惟天地間只有一人的獨愴感。

訴說著，內心熱情不減，獨立而堅強，只是，人都有需要溫暖，需要有人能夠擁抱自己的真實意像。我就是需要愛，需要你。

(4) Patting card

The sky is full of flying snow, and the dead branches are falling. In a vast environment, no one is around, only the falling snow and the whistling wind accompanying me. Silently, it seems there is only one person in the world feeling lonely and sorrow. Saying that the inner enthusiasm is not diminished, I am independent and strong. However, people all need warmth and need real images of being embraced. I just need love and need you.

（五）踩小人卡

無論是在職場上、生活裡，有時真的是處處驚心、粒粒血汗啊！總是會有些姓白名目的傢伙，明明長得眼正嘴闊的，偏偏就不識相非要惹火自己；尤其是自己剛被老闆釘完，上司譙完的心情……真的，不是想甩在地上踩兩下而已。

魅麗纖細的高跟鞋下，無辜的踩住一個……天啊！這種感覺很特別，似乎，自己的心情好轉，優雅與文明立馬回來了呢！

(5) Step-on-the-villain card

Whether in the workplace or in life, sometimes you just have to be on the alert! There will always be some insensitive people who seem to be normal, but they have the tendency to irritate others without knowing it; especially when you are just scolded by the boss... You just wish you could knock down the person on the ground and step on him or her several times.

Under the sleek, high-heeled shoes, guiltlessly stepping on a person... God! The feeling is so special. It seems that my mood is getting better, and my elegant and civilized personalities are coming back!

（六）桃花數

桃花灼夭，媚而多嬌，聞之清雅，望之喜梢。

桃花數卡，本身就是幸福洋溢的代表。以圖像心理學言：是關心，歡聚的來源。以能量論述：粉、桃色能量，能繫人的精力，深植印象。

這張桃花圖卡能撫慰寂寞的心靈，吸引異性的緣分，強化人與人之間的聯繫程度。它的療癒是愉悅和舒服的；能激起內在的溫柔，改變僵化的對待。

(6) Love-attraction (Peach blossom) number

The peach blossom is so charming,

The smell is elegant, and the look is joyful.

The Love-attraction number card itself is the symbol of happiness.

According to the image psychology, it is the source of concern and joy; according to the energy discussions: pink and peach energy can attract people's energy and deeply rooted in their mind.

This Peach blossom card can soothe the lonely soul, attract the fate of the opposite sex, and strengthen the connection between people. Its healing is pleasant and comfortable; it can stimulate the inner gentleness and change the rigid treatment.

（七）宣洩卡

能宣洩情緒，是一種幸福。在這個房間裡，有許多屬於女子的夢幻與心情，掙扎與逃離，無奈與認命；無論是哪一種，都珍貴無比。女人啊！一定要珍愛自己，在宣洩情緒之餘，要記得你手中是握得幸福的。眼前的有，不一定是真有；你以為的無，不一定是沒有。

宣洩不等於失去卻可能失去。所以，圖卡中所表現的放肆與禁錮，正是個人適時放鬆的情緒張力潛在意識。

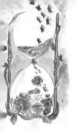

(7) Unbosom card

It is a kind of happiness to be able to release your emotions. In this room, there are many dreams and moods that belong to women, struggle and escape, helplessness and surrender; no matter which one, it is precious. Woman! Be sure to cherish yourself. When you try to release your emotions, remember that you have happiness in your hands.

What is in front of you is not necessarily true; what you think is lost is not necessarily lost. The process of catharsis does not mean you have to lose something, even if it is possible to lose. Therefore, the arrogance and imprisonment shown in the card is the potential consciousness of the emotional tension that the individual relaxes at the right time.

（八）魔鏡卡

「你看我，或許不是我；但我知道，我是我自己。」

每一個人，都有深層的渴望，渴望成為自己想成為那樣的一個人。所以，努力。放棄再努力，努力再放棄，直到找到適合自己的模樣，全心全意可以伸展自己的舞台。

沒有人，生而完美。魔鏡能修飾自己，自信美麗，能照見自己的缺點，督促自己立時改變；更能豐耀自己，讓平日裡不能透露與人說的心事，籍由不斷的自我審視而逐夢成真。

(8) Magical mirror card

"When you look at me, maybe I am not me, but I know, I am myself."

Everyone has a deep desire to be the one they want to be. So, work hard. Give up and try again, try again and give up until you find a suitable appearance that you can extend your stage wholeheartedly.

No one is born to be perfect. The magical mirror can modify you to be confident and beautiful, and it can show your shortcomings, pushing you to change immediately; furthermore, it is able to make you prosper, reveal the unspeakable mind, and make dreams come true through constant self-examination.

（九）風暴卡

風暴來臨，不可預期。即便天旋地轉，身陷其中，我仍一派優雅，無視狂風暴襲。人在漩渦中，卻不被帶離，心境清明，周邊即使黑暗，在我的心裡，依然見藍天白雲。放心！禍患雖不可預期，但是你是光，是自己的主人，一定可以順利通過考驗的。

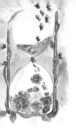

(9) Storm card

The storm is coming, unpredictable. Even I feel as if the sky and earth were spinning around, I am still elegant, ignoring the storm.

I am in the whirlpool, but I am not taken away. My heart is clear, and even if it is dark, I still see blue sky and white clouds in my heart. Rest assured! Although the scourge is unpredictable, you are the light, your own master, and you will pass the test.

（十）災星卡

不要畏懼你無力抵抗災禍的來臨，你有我，我會為你揹負。不要恐懼在大漠之中，看不見歸處，你有我，我會在蒼茫之中帶你走出困境，回到舒適的所在。滿天星藍，流星劃過，點點銀珠成瀑；只要你能堅持，神的力量必定將榮耀歸還給你。

(10) Disaster card

Don't be afraid, you can't resist the coming of the disaster. You have me, and I will bear it for you. Don't be afraid of being in the desert, although you can't see your home, you have me, and I will take you out of the predicament from the vast and return to your comfort zone. In the starry sky, the meteors passed by, just like a waterfall made of silver beads; as long as you can persist, the power of God will return the glory to you.

（十一）逆轉卡

人生不遇難關，是騙人的；這一點不現實。

每個人手上都有一把鑰匙，你可以選擇關上眼前的門也可以選擇打開門。如圖中所呈現通往天堂的道路，每踏上一個階層，就會有一道門，無論是傾斜的門，大門、小門，或是看似輕易就能開啟的門，都要自己親自登上去，親自打開才是。

有人說：神要關上一道門，如何努力你也打不開；神要開啟一道門，你如何想關，你也關不了。這是神對你的考驗，並非祂惡意整你；而是你必須證明自己，證明自己有逆轉改變的力量與決心。記住！鑰匙始終在你自己的手上，無一可奪，也奪不走。

(11) Reverse card

If I say that life is not difficult, it will be a lie, and that is not realistic.

Everyone has a key, you can use it to close the door in front of you, or you can choose to open it. As shown in the picture, on the road to Heaven, every time you go up to a new level, there will be a door, whether it is a sloping one, a big one, a small one, or one that seems to be easy to open, you must try to open it by yourself.

Some people said: If God wants to close a door, you won't have any chance to open it; if God wants to open a door, no matter how hard you try, you can't shut it down. This is God's test for you. It is not that He is malicious to you; it is that you must prove you have the power to reverse and the determination to change. Remember! The key is always in your own hands, and no one can take it from you.

（十二）中貴人卡

「朱雀天門入，鳳凰吉祥飛。」人間孔雀，集兩者之最，富貴而顯。「中貴人」為一官名，中貴人卡為富貴、顯達之意，獲此卡如獲孔雀開屏。

孔雀繪有九尾，尾尾綻放如新生的希望，看見祂，就好像看見百花齊放，處處盎然生機，夢幻，富餘而喜悅。

(12) Noble and superior card

"The Vermilion Bird is at the door of Heaven, and the Phoenix is flying auspiciously." The peacock on earth sets the best of both, rich and dignitary. Chamberlain is a Chinese official title. The Chamberlain card has the meaning of wealth and prosperity, getting this card is like owning a peacock flaunting its tail.

The peacock has nine tails, and the blooming of each tail is like a new hope. Seeing a peacock is like seeing a hundred flowers bloom, everywhere is full of vitality, dreams, affluence, and joy.

（十三）元始卡

在色彩學中，白色、黑色、灰色是屬於無色彩。在大道生於混沌，道法自然衍續的表象中，元始於虛無之境應運而生。

元始，虛無、初始之意。

放下，便立回原點。而這裡的原點，指的不是回到事件或生命的起點，而是不識這個自己的最初。

一切重新開始！由不知這個生命為何，到珍視生命的價值。人，不能改變曾經存在的事實，不能改變過去。

但是可以學習原諒、善待、改變。

原諒自己曾經犯下的錯誤，善待自己健康的活在當下，改變自己的思路，提高自己的視界。

元始卡，有重生之意。無論是誰，得到了這張卡，便得到了救贖。

眼下的自己，正在接受上天的洗禮。洗淨過去一切錯誤，重新迎接彩色人生。

(13) Pre-cosmicstate card

In color science, white, black, and gray are colorless. When the Great Principle born in chaos and in the appearance of the natural evolution of the Tao, the primordial beginning emerged to meet a historic destiny in the world of nihility.

Primordial beginning has the meaning of nihility or emptiness.

Let it go and you will return to the original point immediately. And the original point here is not referring to go back to the beginning of an event or life, but to the outset of not knowing yourself.

Start all over again! From never understand what life means, to cherish the value of life.

You cannot change the facts that existed before and cannot change the past.

But you can learn to forgive, be kind, and change.

Forgive the mistakes you have made, be kind to yourself and live healthy in the present, change your thinking and improve your horizons.

Primordial beginning card has the meaning of a rebirth.

Whoever gets this card will get the redemption.

You are accepting the baptism of heaven at the moment.

Wash away all the mistakes from the past and regain the colorful life.

（十四）幸運卡

北極星映襯九色鹿，其光量不能阻止國色天香的牡丹綻放；夜晚如白晝，九色鹿顯眼前彎路，仍然如大道一般，通暢順行。這樣花好月圓，前途無量，心想事成的幸運，你的人生沒有什麼可以阻擋你，影響你成為更美好的人了。

(14) Lucky card

The nine-color deer is set off by the Polaris, and its light can't stop the bloom of the beautiful peony; the night is like a daytime, although there is a detour in front of the nine-color deer, it is still like an unobstructed boulevard for the deer. What a perfect conjugal bliss, a promising and a lucky future! There is nothing in your life that can stop you and affect you to be a better person.

（十五）異空卡

生命有通則，冥冥之中自有力量在主宰世間，包括時間背後的空域。生有時，死有時，歡笑有時，哭泣有時；心存愛與善的力量，便是穿越時空的鑰匙。相信神，一切困難便得解決。

(15) Savior card

Life has general principles, and there is its own power to dominate the world including a time to be born, a time to die, a time to be happy and a time to weep; the power of love and goodness is the key to crossing time and space. Believe in God, and all difficulties will be solved.

（十六）解憂卡

「我心如鹿，渴慕溪水；我心無憂，如魚得水。」

(16) Solution card

"My heart is like a deer thirsts for stream; my heart is worry-free like fish in the water (very satisfied and pleased)."

國家圖書館出版品預行編目資料

時間神諭：討拍拍舒癒卡／安雪尹編著. --初
版--新竹市：走你文化事業，2020.1
　　面；　公分.
ISBN　978-986-98465-0-9（平裝）
1.占卜 2.心靈療法
292.96　　　　　　　　　　　108018954

時間神諭：討拍拍舒癒卡
Time Oracle: Patting-healing card

作　　者　安雪尹

繪　　者　黃慈

出版發行　走你文化事業
　　　　　300新竹市民生路172號之1

設計編印　白象文化事業有限公司
　　　　　專案主編：陳逸儒　經紀人：徐錦淳

經銷代理　白象文化事業有限公司
　　　　　412台中市大里區科技路1號8樓之2（台中軟體園區）
　　　　　出版專線：（04）2496-5995　　傳真：（04）2496-9901
　　　　　401台中市東區和平街228巷44號（經銷部）
　　　　　購書專線：（04）2220-8589　　傳真：（04）2220-8505

印　　刷　基盛印刷工場

初版一刷　2020年1月

定　　價　1480元

白象文化　印書小舖　PressStore　出版・經銷・宣傳・設計
www.ElephantWhite.com.tw　f 自費出版的領導者　購書 白象文化生活館